SUPER-CHARGED SCIENCE PROJECTS

MAGNETS AND ELECTRIC CURRENT

NOTES

To Parents: Some activities in this book may require the guidance and supervision of an adult to insure the child's safety in handling certain cutting tools suggested for use.

About the Measurement Units Used: Both the U.S. system and the metric system are used in this book. However, the units are not exact conversions. They are approximations, to make measuring easier regardless of what system you use.

THE DEVICES YOU ARE GOING TO MAKE USE BATTERIES

NEVER TRY TO CONNECT THEM TO THE WALL OUTLETS!

YOU COULD CAUSE A SHORT CIRCUIT AND, WORSE STILL, YOU COULD GET HURT.

SUPER-CHARGED
SCIENCE PROJECTS

MAGNETS AND ELECTRIC CURRENT

BARRON'S

THIS IS <u>NOT</u> A SCHOOL BOOK!

There's no need to worry: There aren't any formulas or calculations to do.

We only want you to try your hand at carrying out these activities, all of which you should enjoy greatly.

So, ARE YOU READY FOR A CHALLENGE?

Of course you are. You learn new things better by playing, don't you?

The title of the Spanish Edition is ¿Te Atreves? Imanes Y Corriente Eléctria
© Copyright 1994 by PARRAMON EDICIONES, S.A.
Published by Parramón Ediciones, S.A.,
Barcelona, Spain.

Author: Parramon's Editorial Team

English translation © Copyright 1994 by Barron's Educational Series, Inc.

All inquiries should be addressed to:
Barron's Educational Series, Inc.
250 Wireless Boulevard
Hauppauge, New York 11788

Library of Congress Catalog Card No. 94-72511
International Standard Book No. 0-8120-6436-4

Printed in Spain
4567   9960   987654321

CONTENTS

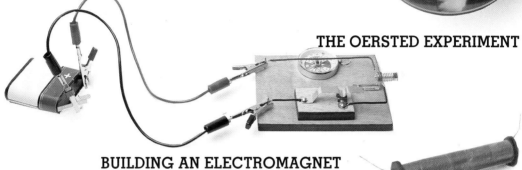

And keep in mind
that words in italics
that are marked
with an asterisk (*)
are explained in
the Glossary at the
end of the book.

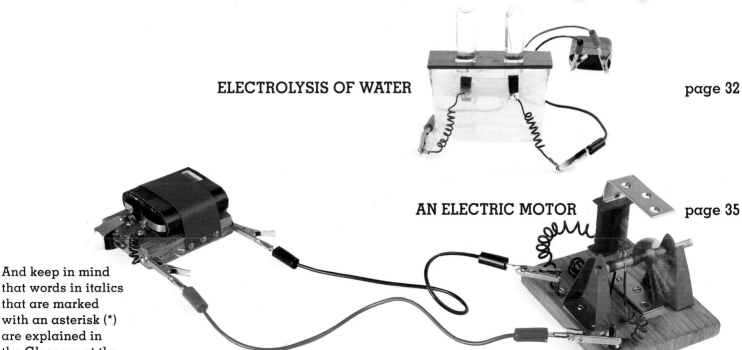

INTRODUCTION

EVERYTHING HAS A BEGINNING

Nowadays, we are so used to electricity that it would be difficult to imagine a world without electric appliances such as stoves, refrigerators, washing machines, heaters, telephones, radios, and televisions. All of these work thanks to electricity. People have learned to exploit the *effects** of electricity throughout recent history.

But the scientific discoveries that led to the mastering of electric energy for its practical use came little by little. Remember, for example, that electric light was invented in 1878, little more than a century ago.

In reality, the full usefulness of electricity was not appreciated until it was discovered that there is a close relationship between the phenomena that magnets display and the electric currents that run along conducting wires. For this reason, all the activities explained in this book—except one—are based on the relationship between magnetism and electricity.

This relationship was discovered at the beginning of the last century by Hans Christian Oersted and André-Marie Ampère.

Hans Christian Oersted (1777–1851), a Danish physicist demonstrated in 1820 that there is a relationship between magnetism and electricity. He proved it by carrying out an experiment that started a new branch of physics, called electromagnetism. The unit of magnetic field strength— the oersted—was named for him.

André-Marie Ampère (1775–1836) was a French mathematician and physicist. He was familiar with Oersted's experiment and decided to explore further the mutual action between magnets and electric currents. The measurement of the intensity of an electric current—the ampere—was named after him.

DID IT ALL BEGIN IN ANCIENT CHINA?

According to certain scholars, around the year 300 B.C. the drivers of the great Chinese merchant caravans discovered the strange behavior of an iron mineral that today we call magnetite.

They knew that by suspending a piece of this substance from a cord and allowing it to swing freely it always came to rest pointing in the same direction. By using this fixed reference they were able to know, at any time, in which direction the caravan was headed. In short: Those ancient travelers used a primitive compass.

It is impossible to know what the first compass in history was like, although we imagine it was much like the one you can see here on this page: A long piece of magnetite suspended from a wooden stick.

LET'S GET TO WORK

A FLOATING MAGNETIC COMPASS

The compass became the sailor's main ally.

But, do you know what the primitive compasses used by sea travelers were like?

If you are curious to find out, you can easily make one yourself.

All you need is a plastic, glass, or ceramic bowl (metal will not do in this case), a flat piece of cork or thin wood, and a small bar magnet.

As you can see in the picture shown here to guide you, the compass we made has a colorful compass card on the lid to make it look nice.

This is the model of the magnetic compass that you will build. It is a fun and easy way to orient yourself, just as those intrepid travelers did so long ago.

To make a primitive compass, float a magnet in a bowl of water.

Whatever the position of the bowl, the magnet will always point approximately north.

HOW TO BUILD A FLOATING MAGNETIC COMPASS

To build a compass similar to the model, you can follow our instructions. Otherwise, you can invent some other setup that will do the same thing. Even an ordinary saucer can be used.

MATERIALS YOU WILL NEED

Some of the materials and tools listed here you may find at home, others can be purchased in a store that sells art supplies:

1. A round plastic container.
2. A container cover, also made of plastic.

3. A piece of sheet cork, polystyrene, or thin wood.
4. A small bar magnet.

5. Paint or markers: Blue, red, and yellow.
6. A sheet of transfer letters.

7. A sheet of transparent acetate.
8. Glue (do not use water soluble glue).

TOOLS YOU WILL NEED

To make the floating magnetic compass, you need:

–A sharp modeler's knife.
–A drawing compass.
–A small brush.
–Drawing materials: Pencil, felt-tipped pen, ruler, and so on.
–Water and a cloth for cleaning the brush.

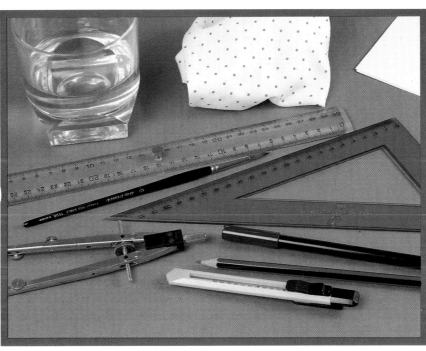

MAKE THE COMPASS IN YOUR OWN WAY, BUT BE INVENTIVE!

It's not necessary to follow our instructions exactly, especially if the container you have is not the same as the one in the book. The following instructions and guidelines will help you to produce your own special compass.

We used an ordinary see-through plastic container with a lid. Try to find something similar.

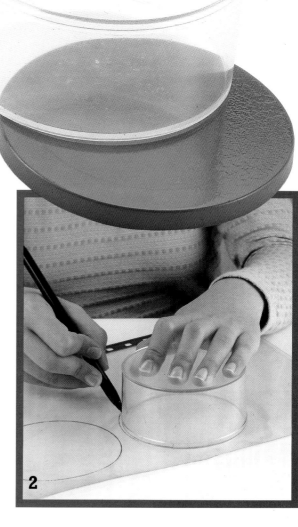

1. Have an adult help you with this step. Draw a circle on the lid, about ¹/₂ inch (1 cm) from the edge. With a cutting tool (and please, be careful!), cut around the inner circle.

2. From the sheet of acetate, cut two circles just big enough to fit inside the lid.

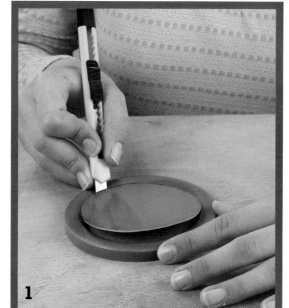

3. And if you enjoy drawing, why not make a colorful compass chart on a piece of white cardboard? We have painted ours blue, red, and yellow. And to mark the points of the compass, we have used transfer letters. Cut out the drawing with scissors and glue it—making sure it is centered— onto one of the see-through circles you have prepared. Use the other circle to cover the face of the drawing for protection.

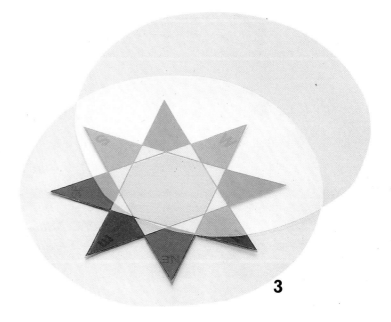

4. Cut out a circle of cork with a diameter that is ¹/₂ inch (1 cm) smaller than the lid of your plastic container. Place the magnet you are going to use in the center of the circle and draw a line around it to mark its position, then paint an arrow pointing outward from either end of the rectangle.

5. Glue the magnet onto the space you have reserved for it, fill the container halfway with water, and float the piece of cork inside it.

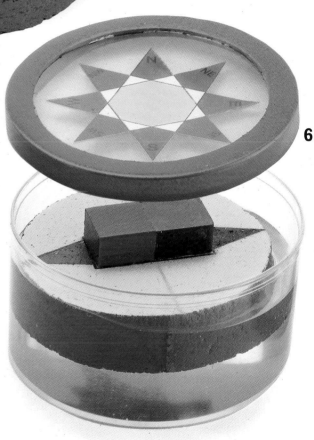

6. Glue the compass chart, face up, inside the lid. Turn the lid to make the N on the chart point the way your compass points.

You are ready to set sail with your compass! Wherever you put it, the floating compass will always point close to a north-south direction. The compass chart marks the other directions.

You are probably asking yourself, What does a magnet have to do with electricity? Don't get impatient, you will soon find out. But first, we are going to demonstrate how an electric current can change a magnet's behavior. Now you have been able to see how any magnet that can turn freely always points to the magnetic north pole.

THE OERSTED EXPERIMENT

At the beginning of this book we mentioned the Danish physicist Oersted and his experiment, which is an important part of the history of science.

Now we will repeat the experiment that Oerstad performed in 1820. It will help you to see that electricity is closely connected to magnetism. But let's go about it step by step.

THE INITIAL SETUP

You will start to work with electricity by first setting up a circuit that you must connect to a battery, something that requires preparation.

FIRST STEP: CONNECTOR WIRES WITH ALLIGATORS!

To set up a temporary electric circuit, you will need a pair of clip leads. A clip lead is simply a length of insulated wire with an alligator clip at each end. An alligator clip has jaws that look like those of an alligator, but the jaws can be opened to fasten on to an electrical terminal. One lead is red (to connect to the positive terminal of the battery) and the other is black (for the negative terminal). You can buy ready-made clip leads or you can prepare them yourself.

There are several different kinds of alligator clips. The instructions on page 13 tell you how to fasten one kind of clip to the end of a wire. If your clips are different, you may still find these instructions helpful because the differences among clips are usually small.

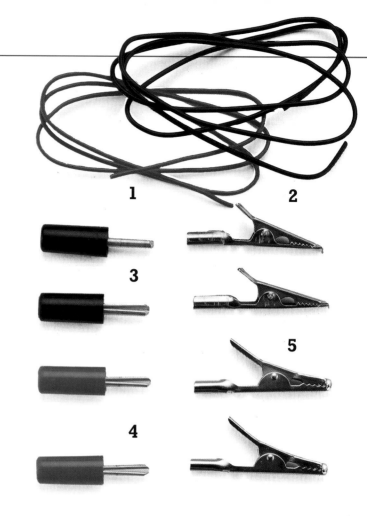

MATERIALS YOU WILL NEED

You can purchase the following materials in most hardware stores:

1. A red connector wire, 1 foot (35 cm) long.
2. A black connector wire, 1 foot (35 cm) long.
3. Two black banana plugs.
4. Two red banana plugs. Ask for the type that doesn't need to be soldered.
5. Four alligator clips with tubular sheaths.
6. A pair of scissors or wire clippers (not shown above).

PREPARING THE LEADS

Stretch out the black and red wires to their full 1-foot (35-cm) lengths.

Remove about 1 inch (25 mm) of the insulating plastic at each end of the wires. Do it as shown in the photographs.

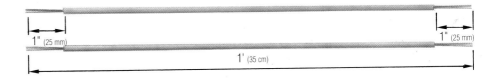

-Using your knife, carefully cut the plastic 1 inch (25 mm) from the end. Don't use too much force or you may cut through the metal wires inside. Cut, slowly and with great care, in a circle around the cable. If you prefer, you can use wire clippers instead.

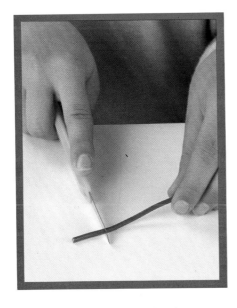

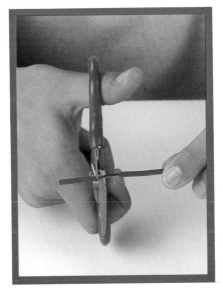

-Using the tips of a pair of scissors, do what you see in the photograph: Grip the section of plastic you have cut and pull it away with the scissors; this will uncover the metal wires.

JOINING THE CLIPS TO THE CONNECTORS

Now attach a banana plug to each end of the wires. See how it is done in the drawings.

-Take the banana plug apart. (1)
-Thread the wire through the insulator.* (2)
-Thread the wire through the ring and wind it around a few turns. (3)
-Finally, insert each banana plug into an alligator clip. (4)

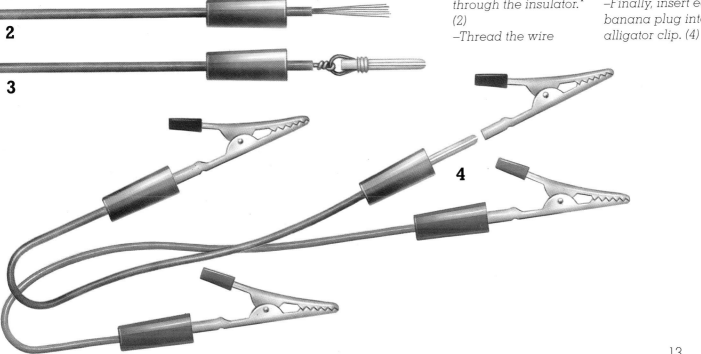

1

2

3

4

SECOND STEP:
SETTING UP A VERY SIMPLE
ELECTRIC CIRCUIT

To repeat Oersted's experiment, you have to set up a very basic electric circuit.

WHAT IS AN ELECTRIC CIRCUIT?

An *electric circuit* is a path through which electric charges can circulate. Of course, the ends of such a circuit must always be connected to a source of electric energy, which may be a *generator** or, in this case, a *battery**.

Batteries—such as the ones you use for making toys or portable radios and cassette recorders work—are *sources** of continuous current produced by chemical means.

In batteries, as in all continuous current sources, there is a *positive* electrode and a *negative* electrode.

A *continuous current* always flows in the same direction: From positive to negative.

We say that a current "leaves" the positive electrode and "enters" the negative electrode, after having traveled the circuit to which the source is connected.

BATTERY TYPES

There are many types of batteries. Two that you surely know are the *wet-cell* battery, which is the kind that starts the motor of a car, and the *dry-cell* battery—the formal name of the battery that powers your toys. All cylindrical batteries of the last kind mentioned provide 1.5 volts (abbreviated, V). In most, the positive

electrode inside them is a carbon bar (with the end covered in metal), while the negative terminal is the metal casing of the battery itself.

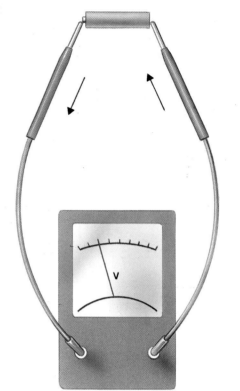

Regardless of their size, dry batteries always produce the same voltage: 1.5 volts.

The 4.5-volt big battery and the 9-volt compact type, in reality, contain several 1.5-volt batteries in a series, where the positive electrode of the first is connected to the negative electrode of the next battery, and so on.

2

+

I

1

3

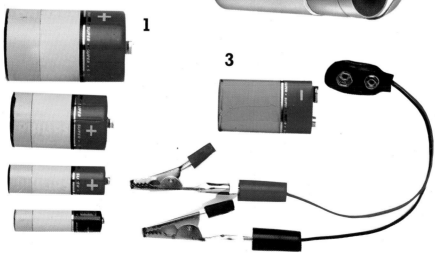

1. All single-cell dry batteries are made to produce 1.5 volts.
2. Here, we have drawn a 4.5-volt battery without its outer

casing so you can see that there are really three cells inside.
3. A 9-volt compact battery. There are six cells inside.

YOUR FIRST CIRCUIT DIAGRAM

For an electric current to create one of its many effects (light, heat, motion), a circuit has to be established. Generally, a circuit consists of:

- A source that produces the current.
- Conductors, or wires, which are the pathways that the current uses to circulate.
- Devices for the desired effect: Bulbs for producing light, resistors for getting heat, or motors for making movement, and so on.

The symbols

To show the electric circuit of a project in a simple way, electricians prepare drawings, called *circuit diagrams*. In these diagrams, they use international symbols to represent the different parts of a circuit.

Shown here are some of these symbols. Use them to draw your first circuit diagram of the basic setup you are about to undertake.

Because doing is a good way of learning, we advise you not to skip this step of the activity.

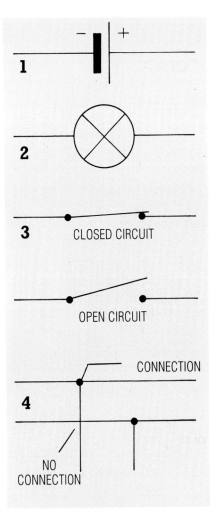

1. This is the symbol that represents a battery. Note that the positive electrode corresponds to the long thin vertical line, while the negative electrode is represented by a short thick line.

2. This symbol is used to represent a light bulb.

3. This symbol shows the switches that are used to open and close a circuit, that is, to enable the current to flow freely (closed circuit) or to interrupt the circulation (open circuit).

4. The conductors are represented by straight lines, and to indicate that two conductors are connected, a dot is inserted at the point of connection.

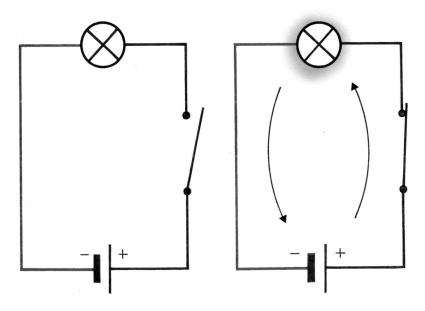

This is a circuit diagram of a basic setup that has a battery, a bulb, a switch and, of course, the conductors that establish the circuit. Note that when the switch is closed the current circulates in the direction shown by the arrows, making the bulb light up. With the switch in the open position, the current cannot flow, therefore, the bulb remains off.

MATERIALS YOU WILL NEED

To make the circuit in your diagram, you can purchase the items listed and illustrated on this page from most home-supply and hardware stores:

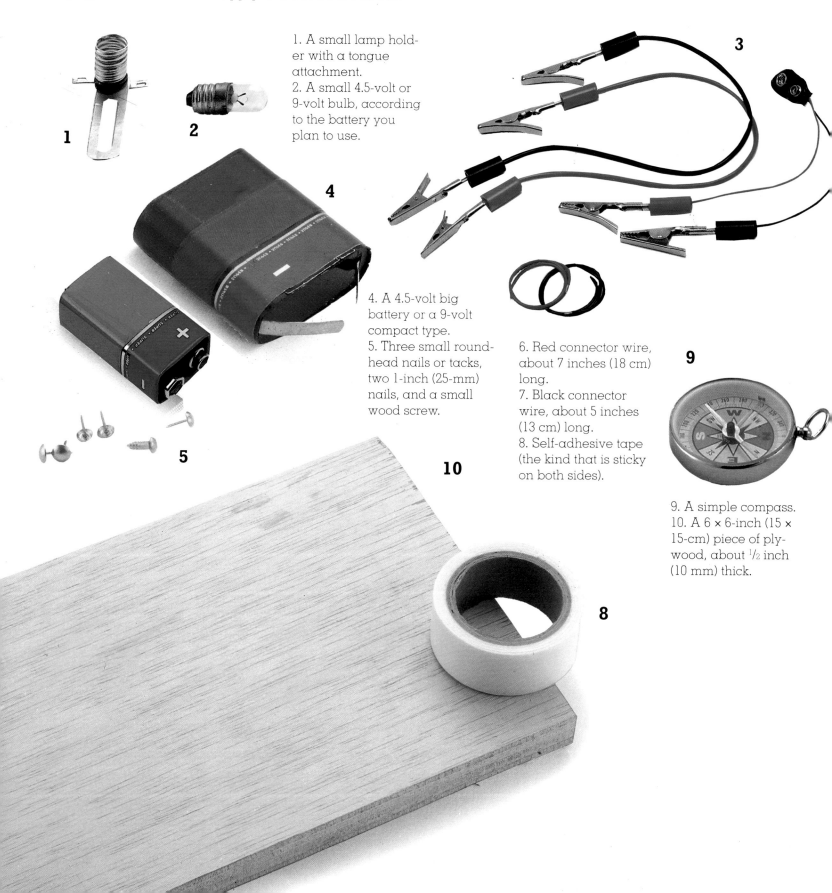

1. A small lamp holder with a tongue attachment.
2. A small 4.5-volt or 9-volt bulb, according to the battery you plan to use.

3. The red and black clip leads you prepared previously (see page 12) or a 9-volt connector with clips at the opposite end of the wires, if you want to use a 9-volt battery.

4. A 4.5-volt big battery or a 9-volt compact type.
5. Three small round-head nails or tacks, two 1-inch (25-mm) nails, and a small wood screw.

6. Red connector wire, about 7 inches (18 cm) long.
7. Black connector wire, about 5 inches (13 cm) long.
8. Self-adhesive tape (the kind that is sticky on both sides).

9. A simple compass.
10. A 6 × 6-inch (15 × 15-cm) piece of plywood, about ½ inch (10 mm) thick.

TOOLS YOU WILL NEED

We recommend that you obtain the tools you see listed and displayed on this page. Tools come in many qualities, to suit all tastes. The ones shown in the photograph, however, are standard and of medium quality (sufficient for your work); they are available in any hardware store.

One tool included in this list is not essential—but it can come in handy when you need to saw, file, or bend metal rods or other such pieces—that is, the *bench vise*. In the illustration, the vise is mounted to the work bench. A small vise is not expensive, and it enables you to do all sorts of things.

1. A pair of combination pliers, which are used for many things: To hold, stretch, and flatten things (with the nose of the pliers); to cut thin wire and string (with the nose blade); to cut thicker wire and string (with the side blade).
2. Small flat-nosed pliers for bending and holding connector wires.
3. Long-nosed pliers, with rounded ends to bend stiff wires and soft pieces of metal into round shapes.
4. Electrician's or kitchen scissors will do.
5. An awl.
6. A small flat-headed hammer.
7. A small vise. (It is not essential, but very useful.)
8. A medium size screwdriver.

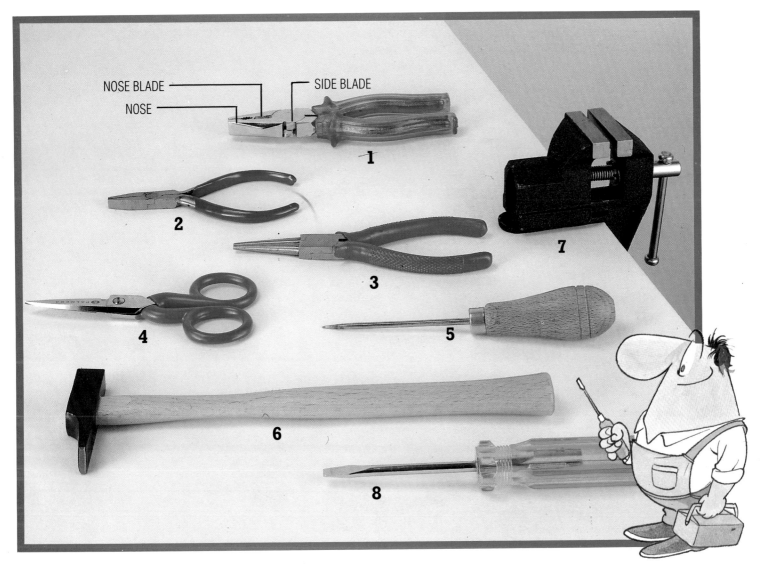

NOSE BLADE — SIDE BLADE
NOSE

1
2
3
4
5
6
7
8

BASES FOR THE CIRCUIT

First, for your safety, before you continue with the experiment, you *must* ask an adult to help you do the sawing and cutting tasks outlined in the following instructions.

Now, begin by cutting two bases for the circuit out of your piece of plywood. Make them similar in size to the ones shown in the drawings. Next, smooth them down with sandpaper.

A small hacksaw (like the one on page 24) is good for sawing plywood. <u>Use it with caution.</u>

BASE 1. The measurements should be, approximately: Length = 2¹/₂ inches (65 mm). Width = 1¹/₂ inches (40 mm). Thickness = ¹/₂ inch (10 mm).

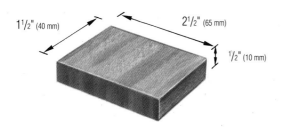

BASE 2. The measurements should be about: Length = 6 inches (150 mm). Width = 4¹/₂ inches (115 mm). Thickness = ¹/₂ inch (10 mm).

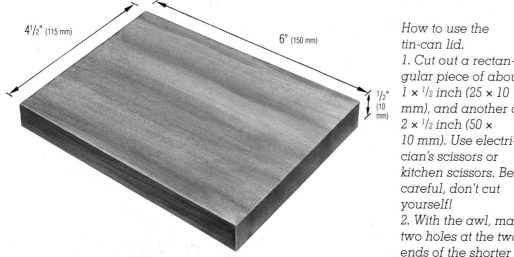

A HOMEMADE SWITCH

You can buy a simple switch very cheaply. But it is much more fun for you to make your own.

You will need the small base you have just prepared, a piece of tinplate (which you can get from the lid of a discarded tin can), and three round-headed nails or tacks.

THE FIXED CONTACT AND THE MOVABLE CONTACT

The switch you are going to make consists of the base and two tinplate contacts—a fixed contact and a movable contact.

FIXED CONTACT

MOVABLE CONTACT

How to use the tin-can lid.
1. Cut out a rectangular piece of about 1 × ¹/₂ inch (25 × 10 mm), and another of 2 × ¹/₂ inch (50 × 10 mm). Use electrician's scissors or kitchen scissors. Be careful, don't cut yourself!
2. With the awl, make two holes at the two ends of the shorter

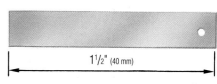

piece, and one hole at only one end of the longer piece.

3. With the aid of the flat- and long-nosed pliers, shape the flat and curved parts of each contact. Follow the shapes shown *in the drawing at right. Look at the illustrations on the next page to see how they should look.*

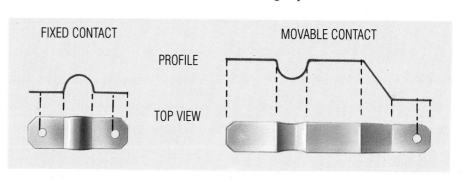

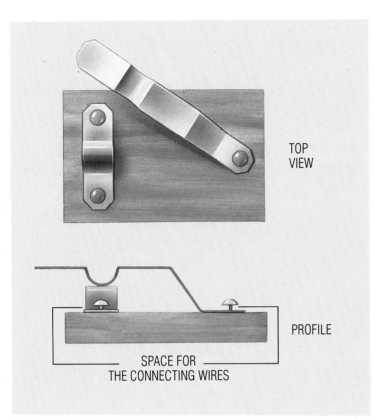

TOP
VIEW

PROFILE

SPACE FOR
THE CONNECTING WIRES

Attach the two contacts to the wood base, as shown. Leave a small space between the head of the nails and the base so you can later wrap a wire around it. Your switch is now ready.

This is roughly what the switch should look like. The wires are attached in the *photograph to let you see why the nails must be driven in only partially.*

A PATH FOR THE ELECTRIC CURRENT

Now that you have all the elements you need for the circuit you can begin to assemble it. As we already mentioned, this is the most basic form of an electric circuit and it is made up of a battery, a switch, and an energy-consuming device—in this case, a light bulb.

So that you have a clear guide as to where each element goes, we will begin these step-by-step instructions with a drawing of the finished circuit board, seen from above.

On page 21, you will find a close-up view of the hookups marked here with the dashed circles.

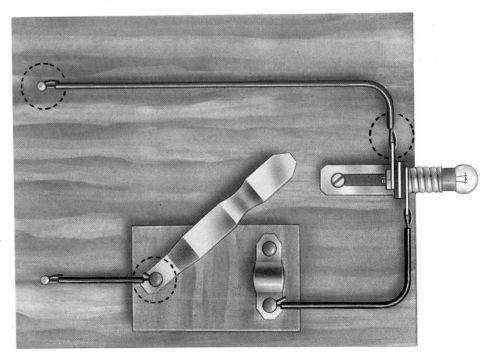

A top view of the circuit board. You can clearly see the position of each element.

INSTALLING THE LAMP HOLDER AND THE SWITCH

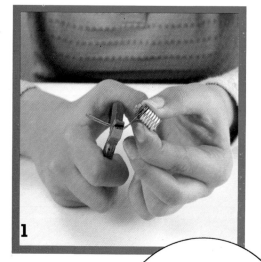

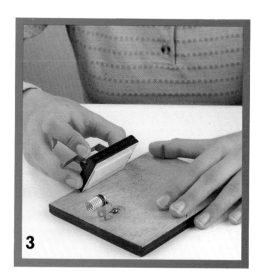

1. Take the lamp holder and fold the tongue as shown in the photograph and drawing. Use the flat-nosed pliers to do this.

2. Using a small wood screw, attach the lamp holder to the large base. Look at the drawing in the previous page (bottom, right) for positioning.

3. Place the switch as shown. To prevent it from moving, you can tack it to the board using a piece of tape (the type that is sticky on both sides).

Later, if you want to use it for another circuit, it will be easy to remove.

WIRING THE CONDUCTORS TO THE LAMP AND TO THE SWITCH

–Hammer two 1-inch (25-mm) nails partway into the board to serve as input and output terminals. Don't bang them in too far; there should be some space left to allow you to connect the alligator clips.

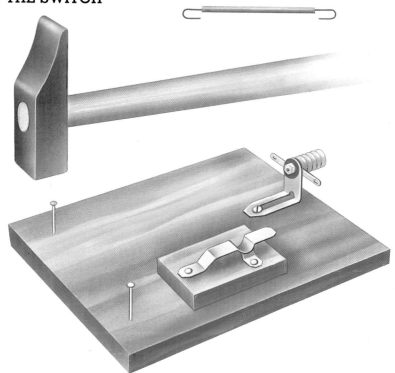

–Calculate the length of wire that each path requires.
–Cut the wire into the three conductors you need.
–Remove about ¹/₂ inch (10 mm) of plastic from the ends of each wire to establish the electric contacts at each connection point.

Here, you can see how the wires are connected to the nails: To tighten the connection, close the loop with the pliers.

–Make the connections to the terminals by wrapping the end of the wire around the nail and then tightening it with the pliers.

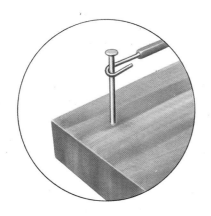

The connections to the lamp holder should be made in exactly the same way: Bend the stripped end of the wire and then tighten it around the terminals with the pliers.

LET'S SEE IF IT WORKS!

Before you try the circuit, make sure all the connections are tight. Retighten the wire-loops connected to the nails and the lamp holder tongue. Then, install the lamp and see how your first circuit board functions:

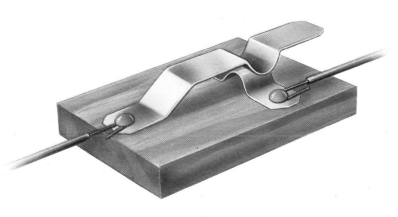

- Connect the battery to the circuit (see illustration, below). The clip of the red leads should "bite" the battery's positive electrode (the short tongue), while the black lead's clip should be connected to the negative electrode (the long tongue).
- Attach each clip at the opposite ends of the leads to the corresponding terminal of the board: Red lead to red terminal, black lead to black terminal.

Your circuit is complete. If all the connections are hooked up correctly, the bulb will light up. When you separate the switch contacts, opening the circuit, the light will go out.

For the switch connections, after hooking up the wires, finish the job by hammering in the nails to assure good contact.

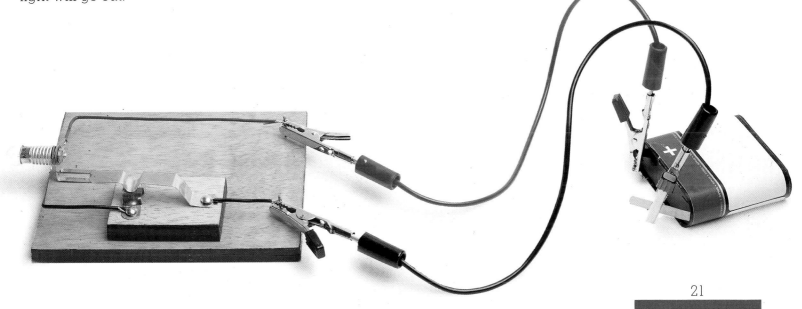

THIRD STEP:
THE OERSTED EXPERIMENT

The first important conclusion you can draw out of this basic circuit experiment is the same one Oersted arrived at almost two centuries ago: The current can flow only if there is a complete path through the whole circuit, including the battery. The current comes out of the positive terminal of the battery, flows through the connecting wires, the bulb, and the switch, and goes back into the battery at the negative terminal. Inside the battery, the circuit is completed as the current flows from the negative terminal to the positive.

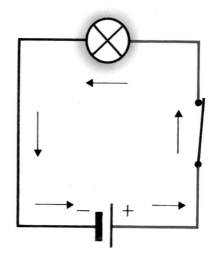

ELECTRICITY AND MAGNETISM LINKED

Now do the following: With the switch open, place your compass below the longest of the connecting wires, aligning north and south with the direction of the wire, as shown in the picture. Then, turn the compass until the compass needle also lines up with the wire.

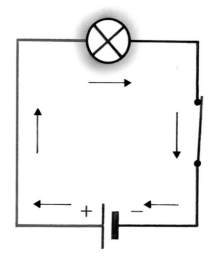

A continuous current flows from the negative electrode to the positive inside the battery, and from the positive to the negative terminals of the circuit wires.

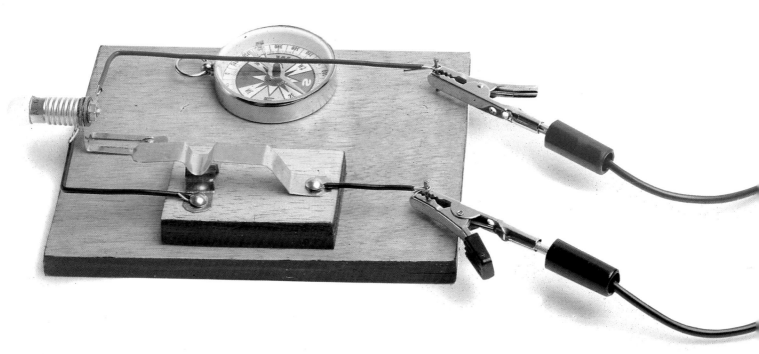

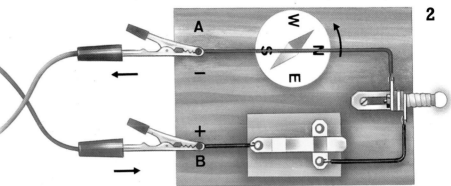

1

2

Close the circuit (the lamp will go on) and look at what happens to the compass:
–If, as in drawing 1, the positive lead is in terminal A, the needle will turn to the right. Did you see it?
Now, with the circuit open (the lamp should be out) invert the circuit's polarity, as shown in drawing 2.

That is, connect the battery's positive electrode (red lead) to the board's black terminal, B; then, the negative electrode (black lead) to the board's red terminal, A.
–With the positive lead in terminal B, the compass's needle should this time turn to the left, instead of to the right.

Observe: The position of the board's elements is the same as before, but the compass has turned in the opposite direction.

The change in polarity of the *electric field** has reversed the direction of the current, which in turn reversed the magnetic field affecting the magnetized needle.

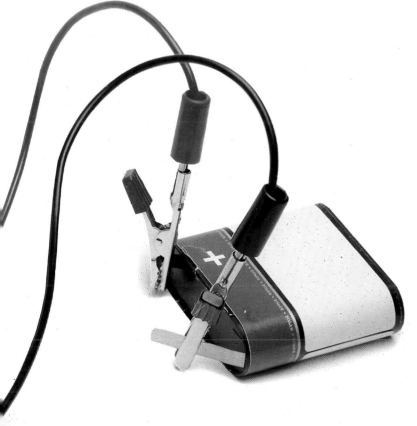

WHY DOES THE NEEDLE TURN?

Here is the second important matter we can deduce from this experiment:

As you know, due to the earth's *magnetic field**, a magnet that can rotate freely comes to rest in a north-south direction, and it only changes when there are other forces at play that are independent of the earth's magnetic field.

So: *The movement that a compass's magnetic needle undergoes every time an electric current passes nearby, tells us that a magnetic force exists around the conductor wire.* The direction of this *force field** changes every time the direction of the current is reversed.

This discovery played a vital role in the history of science and technology. Oersted paved the way for the study of electromagnetic phenomena and their applications, which include electromagnets, transformers, electric motors, dynamos, and alternators.

BUILDING AN ELECTROMAGNET

You have shown how an electric current creates a magnetic field around the conductor it is flowing through. Well, now we are going to show how an electric current can change a *temporary magnet** into a iron bar that behaves like a *permanent magnet** which attracts iron and always indicates north and south when it is allowed to spin freely, like the needle of a compass.

ADDITIONAL MATERIALS AND TOOLS

This demonstration is easy but, to work efficiently, you need two additional tools and some new materials. You can see photographs of them on this page.

1. Sticky tape or clear tape, ½ inch (12.7 mm) wide. A small roll is enough.

1

2. Enameled copper wire, 0.5 millimeters in diameter. You can buy it in rolls from stores that sell electronic materials.

2

3. A small metal file, flat on one side and rounded on the other.

3

4. A small metal saw. The one you see here is a hacksaw, which is inexpensive and allows you to use blades of different thicknesses for cutting either metal or wood.

4

5. Wrought iron bar, about ⁵⁄₁₆ inch (8 mm) in diameter. A piece 3 inches (75 mm) long is sufficient.

5

24

FIRST STEP:
PREPARING THE IRON CORE
FOR THE ELECTROMAGNET

All electromagnets are made of two basic elements: An iron core and a coil; coils are almost always made from copper wire, wound around the core.

The core of your small electromagnet will consist of a wrought iron bar, about 3 inches (75 cm) long and $^{5}/_{16}$ inch (8 mm) in diameter. One millimeter more, or less, will make no difference.

1. Under adult super-vision, clamp the bar firmly into the bench vise and saw off a 3-inch (75-mm) length. In cutting, try to keep the saw vertically straight so that the cut is even.

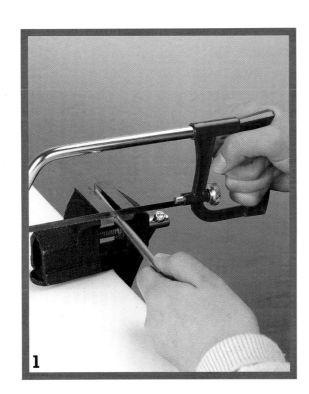

2. If these cuts turn out slanted, you can correct them with a few strokes of the file. Look at the photograph and do the same.

The end to be filed should stick out only a little above the level of the vise. Holding the file with both hands is safer and more efficient.

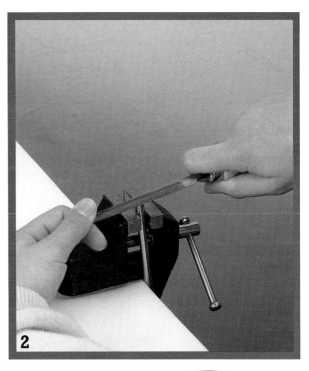

3. Wrap the clear tape around the iron core, leaving about $^{1}/_{4}$ inch (5 mm) uncovered at each end.

The binding should be only one layer thick. If you make it any thicker, your electro-magnet will be weaker.

The tape will prevent any electrical contact between the core and the coil that would produce a short circuit.*

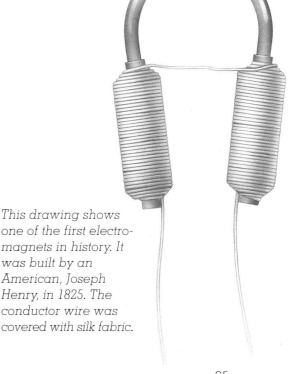

This drawing shows one of the first electro-magnets in history. It was built by an American, Joseph Henry, in 1825. The conductor wire was covered with silk fabric.

SECOND STEP: THE COIL

Now you have to wind the coil around the core of your electromagnet. It is not a difficult task, but pay close attention to the points highlighted in boldface in the following instructions.

4. Cut out two small cardboard rings (the measurements are given in the drawing) and place one over each end of the iron bar. Don't forget the small hole for the wire.

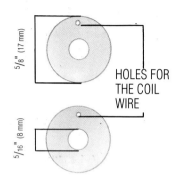

5/8" (17 mm)

HOLES FOR THE COIL WIRE

5/16" (8 mm)

4

5. Using the enameled copper wire, wind 150 to 200 turns along the core you have prepared. **The wire must be wound tightly against the core and close together.**

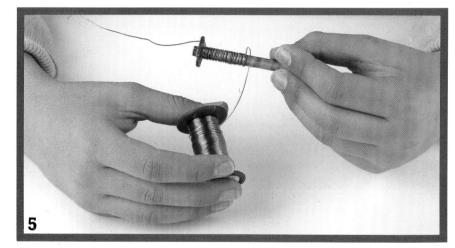

5

It is important to leave a 2-inch (5-cm) length of wire at the beginning and end of the coil. *Pull these ends through the small holes in the cardboard rings.*

6. To protect the coil, cover it with one or two layers of clear tape. If you want an even better appearance, add a cardboard cylinder around the electromagnet's coil.

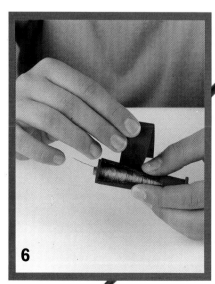

6

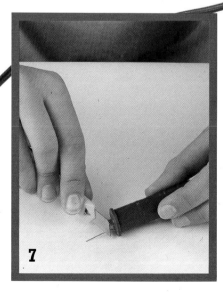

7

7. **Don't forget this step:** *Using sandpaper, or a modeler's knife (but be careful with your fingers!), scrape the ends of the coil wire to remove the insulating enamel layer that covers it. If you didn't do this, there would be no electrical contact at the coil ends.*

8. You'll need to connect the magnet to a battery. From your supply of wire, cut two 5-inch (13-cm) lengths (one black and one red). Strip about ¼ inch (5 mm) of insulation at one end of each wire and attach a connector terminal* (see drawing in Glossary) to each wire. Now, carefully insert the ends of the electromagnet wire, which you scraped free of enamel, into the unstripped ends of your connecting wires.

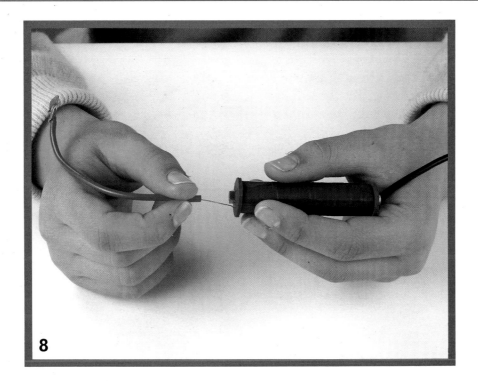

8

DOES IT WORK?

To be complete, your electromagnet needs an electric current. Thus, set up the circuit you see in the illustration, below. Use your 4.5-volt big battery (not shown) as well as the clip leads and switch from the circuit board you made earlier. And remember to leave the switch in the open circuit position.

Next, get some thumb tacks, small nails, clips, pins, or other small objects and place them near your magnet. You will see that:

CONCLUSION

The previous experiment with the compass and this one with the small electromagnet both show that an electric current can produce a magnetic field. Thus, while the current is flowing through the conductor coil, the iron in the electromagnet has the same properties as a permanent magnet.

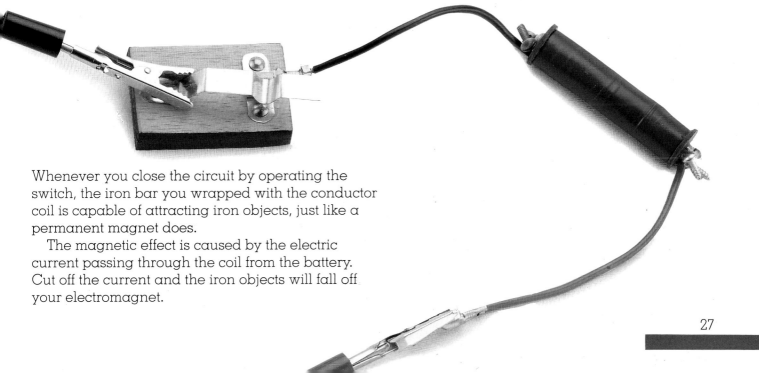

Whenever you close the circuit by operating the switch, the iron bar you wrapped with the conductor coil is capable of attracting iron objects, just like a permanent magnet does.

The magnetic effect is caused by the electric current passing through the coil from the battery. Cut off the current and the iron objects will fall off your electromagnet.

A MORE POWERFUL ELECTROMAGNET

You have succeeded in the previous experiments, so maybe now you would enjoy a small challenge. Here are all the details you need to make another, more powerful magnet. But we do warn you, this job is rather more complicated because it requires a steady hand and a little patience.

You are going to build a *horseshoe magnet*, which takes its name from the shape of the iron core.

FIRST STEP:
THE IRON CORE

1. Cut a 7-inch (180-mm) length from the iron bar you used for your first electromagnet. (Remember, using the hacksaw requires adult supervision.) As we mentioned before, try to cut straight by keeping the saw perpendicular to the iron bar. After you have cut it, make a mark 2¹/₂ inches (65 mm) from each end.

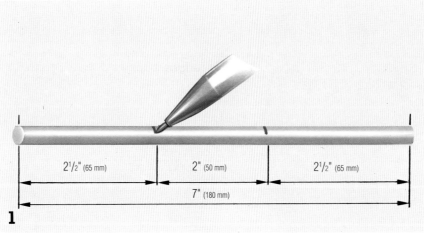

2. Now you might need the help of someone strong, because you'll have to bend the bar into the shape you see in drawing 3. The photograph shows how a bench vise makes this operation easier:
a) Clamp the bar firmly into the vise, so that 2¹/₂ inches (65 mm) sticks out above the mark.
b) Pulling downward with a pair of combination pliers, you can bend the bar without too much difficulty.

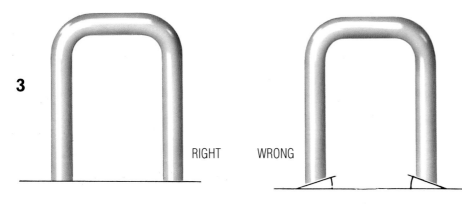

RIGHT   WRONG

3. So that the electromagnet loses none of its power, it's important that both poles should lie in the same plane, as you can see in the drawing.

SHOW HOW SKILLFUL YOU ARE!

SECOND STEP:
THE SPOOLS FOR THE COILS

Now you have to make two spools for easier winding of the copper wire around the two conductor coils. So you need two identical spools of the size shown in the drawing.

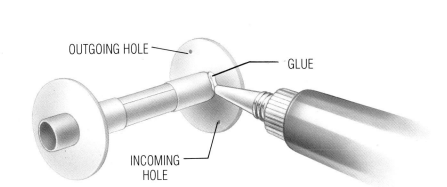

STRIPS OF CLEAR TAPE

BEND

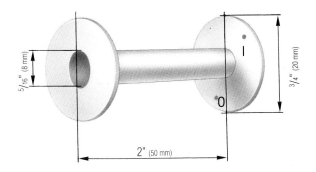

OUTGOING HOLE

GLUE

INCOMING HOLE

Do as follows:

–Cut two thin cardboard rectangles, 2 × ³/₄ inches (50 × 20 mm), and, on another piece of thicker cardboard, draw four washers like the ones in the drawing.

Carefully cut them out and make two small holes very near the edge in two of them. Mark one with an I (incoming) and the other with an O (outgoing).

–To assemble the spools, roll the cardboard rectangles, one at a time, around the iron bar, joining the edges with two strips of clear tape. Take the resulting tube off and glue washers to the ends of the tube. One end should have an I–O washer.

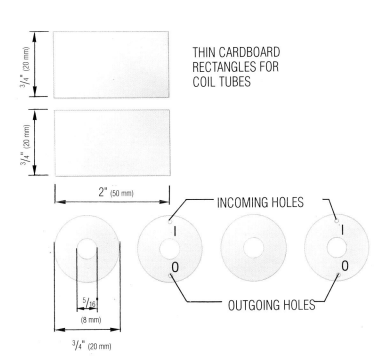

THIN CARDBOARD RECTANGLES FOR COIL TUBES

INCOMING HOLES

OUTGOING HOLES

THIRD STEP:
THE COILS

To make your electromagnet, you have to wind 300 turns of wire around each spool. A few more or less will not matter, but if you use a great deal less, the wire will overheat and may burn out.

With a given core, the strength of an electromagnet depends on how many turns of wire there are in the coil and on how much current flows through them. You might think you can make the magnet stronger by winding more turns, but this does not work very well. The reason is that when the wire is longer, the current is smaller. Whatever you gain by adding turns is lost because of the reduction in current. To make the magnet stronger, you have to increase the current. You can do this is by using either thicker wire or a higher-voltage (4.5V) battery.

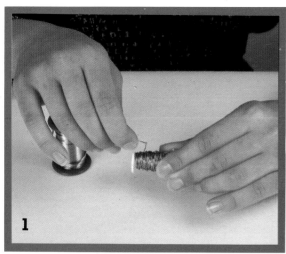

1

THE COILS

1. With sandpaper, remove the enamel from about ¹/₂ inch (10 mm) off the end of the copper wire you are going to use and thread this end through the incoming hole (I) on one of the two spools. Let some of the wire stick out about 2 inches (5 cm) from the cardboard washer. Now you can start to wind the wire, but slowly. Try to keep the turns very tight together, one next to the other so that they are evenly distributed.

2-INCH (5-CM) END

O

I

2

FLEXIBLE WIRE

PLASTIC "MACARONI" (TUBE)

3

TERMINAL

4

3. Place the spools on the core, one on each parallel section. Then connect the O-end of one of the spools to the I-end of the other. If you protect this connection with a plastic "macaroni,"—as the insulator is commonly called—all the better. Although not entirely necessary, it makes for a better finish.

4. You can also connect the remaining ends of the coils to connecting wires with connector terminals, as you did with your first electromagnet. This gives you a better finish and makes the battery connection easier.

2. When you have counted 300 turns, cut the wire (again, leaving 2 inches (5 cm) at the end) and thread it through the outgoing hole (O). Now, to protect the copper wire, wrap clear tape over the coil, then cover it with a rolled up piece of cardboard. We've also added a wrapping of colored tape. Repeat the process for the other coil.

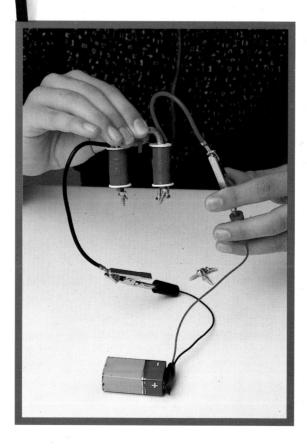

READY!

Now you can connect your horseshoe electromagnet to a 4.5-volt battery, or even better, a 9-volt one. As always, your clip leads are the best method. You will discover that this electromagnet is much more powerful than the first. The one we made can lift pieces of iron weighing up to 10¹/₂ ounces (300g).

IT'S THE IDEAS THAT COUNT!

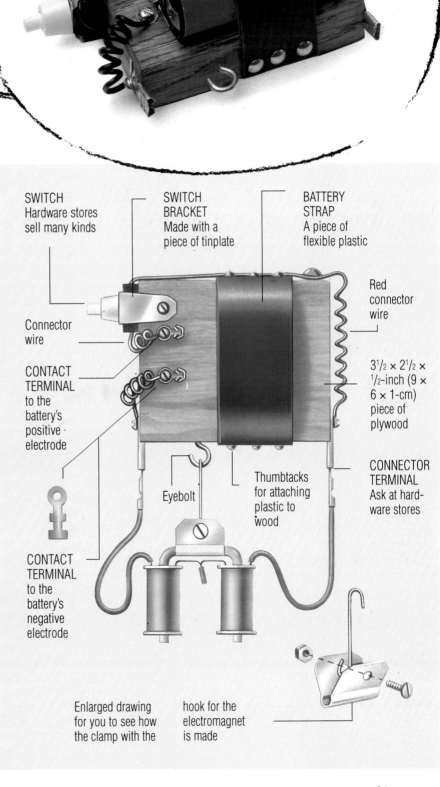

SWITCH
Hardware stores sell many kinds

SWITCH BRACKET
Made with a piece of tinplate

BATTERY STRAP
A piece of flexible plastic

Connector wire

Red connector wire

CONTACT TERMINAL
to the battery's positive electrode

$3^1/_2 \times 2^1/_2 \times ^1/_2$-inch (9 × 6 × 1-cm) piece of plywood

Eyebolt

Thumbtacks for attaching plastic to wood

CONNECTOR TERMINAL
Ask at hardware stores

CONTACT TERMINAL
to the battery's negative electrode

Enlarged drawing for you to see how the clamp with the hook for the electromagnet is made

Our clever friend has found that, when it comes to "playing" with his electromagnet, clip leads aren't very practical. So he thinks and thinks and then has a great idea! Why not build a battery holder with a switch to connect and disconnect the battery, without having to attach and remove the clips all the time?

HERE'S HIS IDEA

ARE YOU READY FOR A CHALLENGE?

ELECTROLYSIS OF WATER

Water is a conductor of electricity. This means that an electrical current can run through it. For this reason, it is dangerous to handle electrical devices when your hands are wet.

But danger aside, something interesting happens when an electric current is sent through a body of water: A process called *electrolysis* takes place.

DO YOU KNOW WHAT ELECTROLYSIS IS?

The word "electrolysis" is made up of two Greek words: *electron*, or electricity, and *lysis*, which means to separate or break up. Therefore, electrolysis is the separation of *elements** that make up a compound, by means of an electric current.

In this experiment, you are going to make a device that separates water into the elements that make up the water compound.

The effect is chemical, of course, not one of electromagnetism. However, we think you will enjoy observing one of the most characteristic and important effects produced by an electric current.

MATERIALS YOU WILL NEED

To conduct the electrolysis experiment, you will need the following items, as shown in the photograph above right.

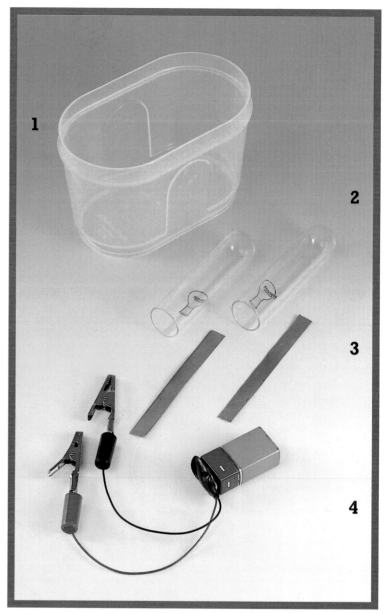

1. A glass or plastic container.

2. Two glass or plastic tubes, about 6 inches (15 cm) long by ⅝ inch (1.5 cm) in diameter.

3. Two pieces of copper, approximately 4 × ½ inches (10 × 1 cm).

4. A 9-volt battery with clip leads; if you want, you can add coiled connector wires with *connector terminals** at one end.

In addition, you will need electrician's tape and a 2-foot (60-cm) long piece of small plastic or rubber tubing. This last item is available at hardware or aquarium supply stores.

The instructions that follow are based on the shape and size of the container we have used. But you can adapt the idea to any other kind of container.

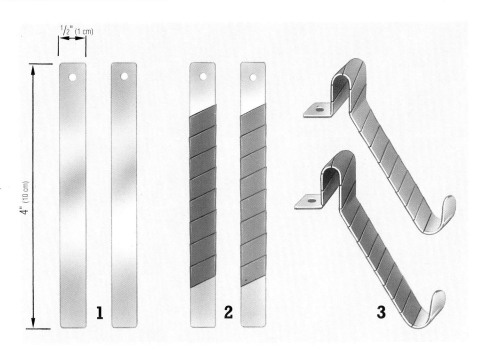

SHAPING THE ELECTRODES FOR YOUR ELECTROLYSIS DEVICE

1. Taking care not to cut yourself, start by cutting two pieces of copper about 4 inches (10 cm) long by ¹/₂ inch (1 cm) wide, and make a small hole at one end.
2. Cover these two metal strips with

insulating tape, leaving approximately ¹/₂ inch (1 cm) uncovered.
3. Bend the two electrodes into the shape you can see in the drawing, at right. Use your flat-nosed pliers to do this.

MOUNTING THE GLASS TUBES

4. Cut a piece of thick cardboard into the shape shown in the drawing. If your container is different from ours, the cardboard piece

should be big enough to entend over the edges of your container. The holes should be just the right size to hold your tubes firmly.

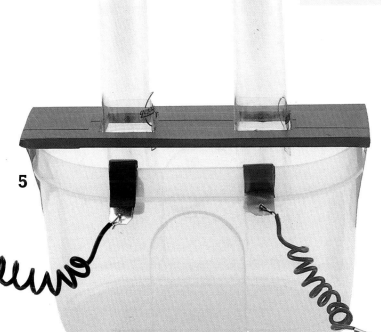

5. Pass a tube through each of the holes. The open ends of the tubes should project far enough to reach well down into your container.

Fill the container nearly to the top with water. Add a pinch of salt and stir; salt makes the water a better conductor of electricity.

Mount your copper electrodes by hooking the end with the hole onto the side of the container. The other end of each must project into the open end of a tube. You may have to adjust the shape of the electrodes to make them fit.

CONNECTIONS

To complete the setup, fill the glass tubes with the water. Do this the way the girl in the picture does: Run the rubber tube through the water and up to the very top of each glass tube. Suck the air out of the glass tubes, one at a time, just as if you were sipping soda through a straw. Fill both tubes to the very top.

Using your clip leads, connect the copper electrodes to the terminals of the battery. Now, observe what happens: Small bubbles begin to form on the end of the electrodes inside each tube; they then rise up through the water and occupy the upper space, forcing the liquid downward. After a while, you'll see that the gas that forms on the positive electrode, which is hydrogen, takes up twice as much space as the gas that forms on the nega-tive electrode, oxygen. This is one way of showing that water has twice the number of hydrogen mole-cules for each one of oxygen. That's why the *chemical formula** for water is H_2O.

In conclusion, an electric current can separate the water molecules into its elements: Two parts hydrogen, one part oxygen.

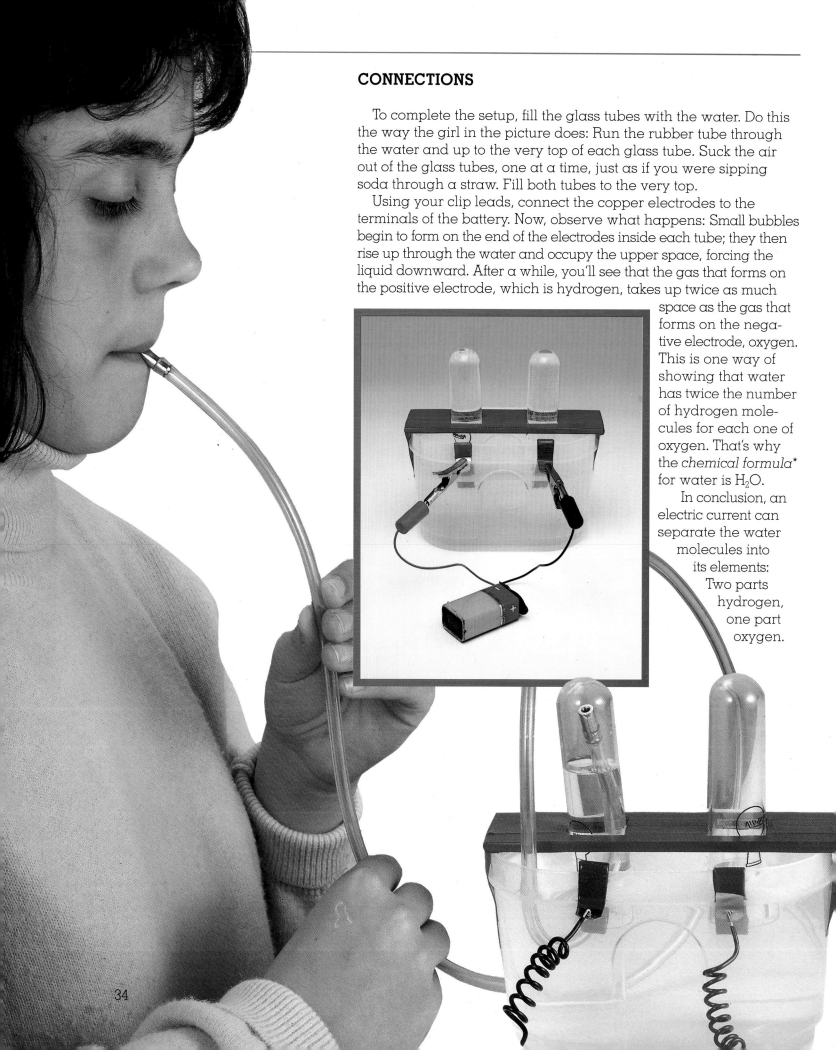

AN ELECTRIC MOTOR

For this project, the last in the book, you *must* enlist the help or guidance of an adult because it requires the cutting and sawing of some metal parts.

Step by step, you are going to build a simple electric motor, but one with all the basic components that go into every such motor, big and small.

You can build this motor without "professional" materials or specialized tools. However, you will need a few things, among them: Plenty of curiosity, patience, and—most important of all—enthusiasm!

ARE YOU READY FOR A CHALLENGE?

MATERIALS AND TOOLS

Gather the tools that you have been using up to now. Additionally, because the diameter of a hole may need enlarging, you will find that a small "rat-tail" file might be handy.

And, here is the list and a photograph of the materials we used:

1. Two 2½-inch (65-mm) angle brackets, about ¾ inch (20 mm) wide. (We bought ours in a hardware store.)
2. A 6¼-inch (160-mm) bar of wrought iron, approximately ⁵/₁₆ inch (8 mm) in diameter.
3. A wooden board, approximately 4¾ × 4 × ⁵/₈ inches (120 × 100 × 15 mm) in size.
4. About 66 feet (20 m) of enameled copper wire; 0.5 mm in diameter, more or less.
5. Plastic insulating tape.
6. A small piece of tin-plate. (You can use the discarded lid of a tin can.) If possible, also a piece of thin copperplate.
7. Two connector terminals. (We used the terminals of a broken plug.)
8. Red and black single-strand wire, a length of 3 inches (75 mm) each.
9. A piece of cardboard or stiff plastic.
10. Thirteen screws and washers (not shown).

"Rat-tail" files are particularly helpful for enlarging the diameters of holes on metal when they are too small.

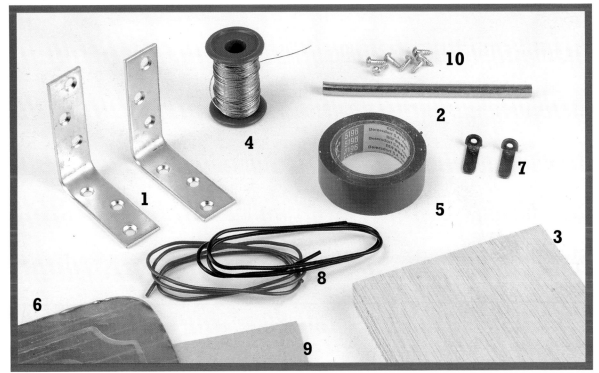

FIRST STEP: BUILDING THE STATOR FOR THE MOTOR

In case you didn't know, the *stator* of a motor is the set of components that make up the non-moving part of the motor, that is, the part that doesn't turn.

The stators of electric motors have an iron core with one or more coils. Therefore, when they are supplied with electricity, they act like an electromagnet. The stators of many small motors use a permanent magnet instead of an electromagnet. So you have two options:

1. Build a stator with a coil, which is what we are going to do.

2. Use a permanent magnet in the stator. (We'll show you one later.)

Ready? Look carefully at the drawings and photographs but above all, use your ingenuity. And remember that you can always use other angles for your stator, or even make them out of tin.

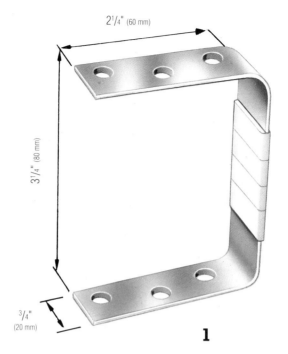

1. Take the two angle brackets and lay them on one side. Attach them by overlapping and binding them tightly with insulating tape, as you can see in the drawing. The distance between their ends, for the motor that we built, is about 3¼ inches (80 mm), but it can be a little more or less depending on the angle irons you're using.

1

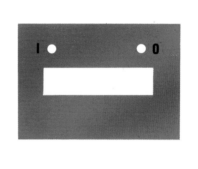
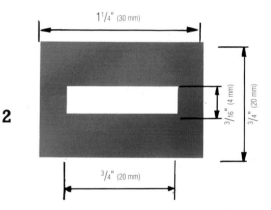

2

2. Cut out two pieces of cardboard shaped as in the drawing. They will be the end pieces of the coil you are going to add to the core you have just made with the brackets. Note that the measurements of the cutout must be exact so as to fit the vertical section of the core. And don't forget the two small holes to thread the coil wires through.

3. Slip the two cardboard parts, one over each end of the core, and attach them with glue about ¾ inch (20 mm) from each elbow. Before proceeding to the second step, wait until the glue is good and dry. Don't get impatient! You wouldn't want your coil to fall apart.

If, like us, you like things to look nice, before gluing them in place, you can paint both pieces of cardboard in your favorite color.

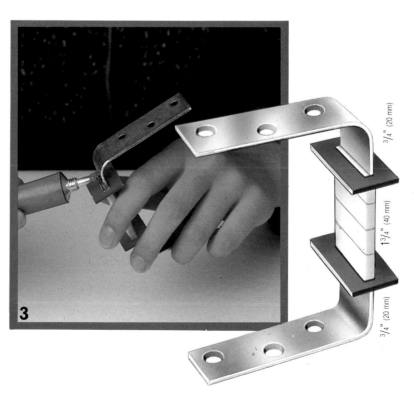

3

SECOND STEP: WINDING THE COIL

1. Use sandpaper to remove the enamel from the tip of the wire you are going to use, thread it through the incoming hole (I), letting about 4 inches (10 cm) stick out. Now you can start winding the coil!

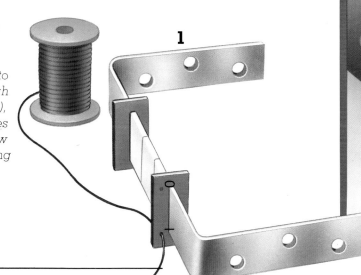

4" (10 cm) END

SCRAPE OFF ENAMEL

3. When you've counted the 400 turns, cut the wire, but remember to leave enough free wire to have another 4-inch (10-cm) end after threading it through the outgoing hole (O). Remove the enamel from the tip of this end, too.

4" (10 cm) END

SCRAPE OFF ENAMEL

THIRD STEP: BUILDING THE ROTOR PARTS

Now comes the more complicated part of this assembly. We are warning you so that you'll use your tools safely and pay close attention to the drawings and photographs for accuracy. Remember, a picture is worth a thousand words.

Follow the process as we explain it, step by step, on the next page, and you'll see how it turns out well.

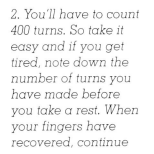

2. You'll have to count 400 turns. So take it easy and if you get tired, note down the number of turns you have made before you take a rest. When your fingers have recovered, continue winding. (Actually, 10 turns more or less are not going to affect the performance of the motor. What is important is that you wind the wire tightly and closely together, as we mentioned earlier.)

4. In this photograph, you can see the stator for your motor, ready to be attached to its base. As before, we have protected the coil wire with plastic insulating tape. (Because we like our work to have a nice finish, we used colored tape.)

1. With the supervision of an adult, use the hacksaw to cut the section of iron bar that is going to be the shaft of the motor. Make it about 3½ inches (90 mm) long. You already know how to do this, don't you? Cut another two lengths of bar. These should be 1⅜ inches (35 mm) long. We shall call them "rotor blades."

2. You'll need two pieces of tinplate, 2¾ × ¼ inches (70 × 7 mm), which will be the "rotor blade supports." Draw the outlines using a felt-tip pen, on the tinplate (or you can use the clean, flat lid of a discarded sardine tin can). Cut them out with the scissors, again, under adult supervision. You'll be safer if you wear a pair of old gloves. Remember, the edges are very sharp.

3. Don't put the scissors away, because now

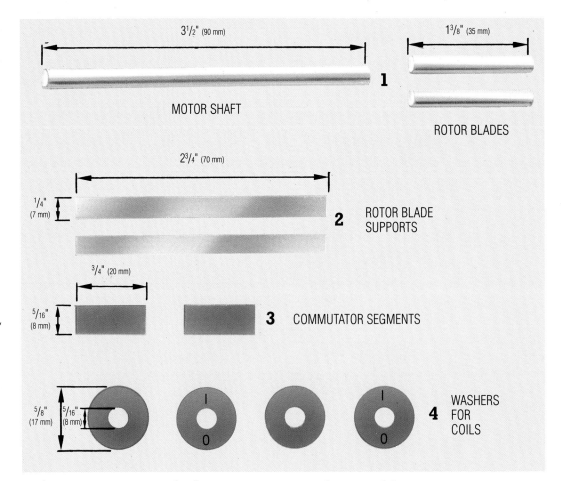

3½" (90 mm)

MOTOR SHAFT

1

1⅜" (35 mm)

ROTOR BLADES

2¾" (70 mm)

¼" (7 mm)

2 **ROTOR BLADE SUPPORTS**

¾" (20 mm)

5/16" (8 mm)

3 **COMMUTATOR SEGMENTS**

⅝" (17 mm) 5/16" (8 mm)

4 **WASHERS FOR COILS**

you're going to prepare two small pieces, ¾ × 5/16 inch (20 × 8 mm), using the same tinplate or a very thin copperplate. They're going to be the "commutator segments."

4. Make four cardboard or plastic washers, using the sizes shown in the drawing. Don't forget that two of them must have an incoming and an outgoing hole for the copper wire from the rotor coil.

5. Last, prepare some very thin strips of insulating tape. You'll need them to insulate different parts of the rotor and to attach the commutator segments to the shaft. To do this, place a 4-inch (10-cm) length of insulating tape on a flat piece of wood and, as you can see in the photograph, cut thin strips using the modeler's knife and a ruler. You can peel these strips off the wood as you need them.

5

FOURTH STEP:
ASSEMBLING THE ROTOR PARTS

Now, note the order of the drawings on this page. You must follow exactly the same sequence when assembling the parts of the rotor:

1 **A**

1. Sandwich one of the blades between the two rotor blade supports (see drawing A). Let the bench vise hold your parts "sandwich," while you tightly bind the parts together with your precut strips of insulating tape. (Look at the photograph.) Next, insert the other blade

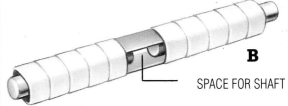

B

SPACE FOR SHAFT

between the blade supports at the opposite end, but leave sufficient space in the middle for the rotor

shaft to pass through snugly. Bind this side with tape as well. (See drawing B.)

2. Insert the rotor shaft in the gap between the two blades. Make sure it fits in tightly and, to secure it better, add a few more turns of binding near the shaft, at both

sides. Look at drawing C and note that the two sections of shaft are not equal in length: One is 1³/₈ inches (35 mm) and the other is 1³/₄ inches (45 mm).

2

1³/₈" (35 mm)

1³/₄" (45 mm)

C

3

D

3. Now you can make the rotor coils. Begin by firmly gluing the cardboard washers in place. (See drawing D.) Note that the washers with the I- and O-holes go next to the shaft.

4. Wind 200 turns of wire around each of the blades to form the coils. With the practice you gained in building your horseshoe electromagnet, this task should give you no trouble. But refer to drawing E and note the following details:

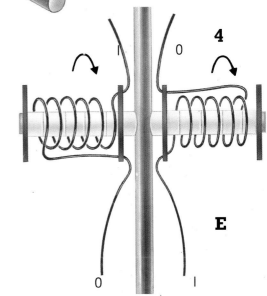

0   **4**

E

0   I

—The wire of both coils must be wound in the same direction. —The ends of the wire, both at the beginning and the end of the

coils, should be about 2 inches (5 cm) long. As you already know, you'll have to remove the enamel from the ends with sandpaper.

FIFTH STEP:
BUILDING THE COMMUTATOR

The "commutator," mounted on the shaft, is the part of the motor that receives the electric current that drives it. The current—picked up by the parts called "segments," which in turn receive it from two fixed parts called "brushes"—passes to the rotor coils.

Look carefully at the drawings. Drawing A shows an enlarged view of the coils and the rotor shaft so that you can see more easily what you have to do. Drawing B is a detail of the shaft end that carries the commutator.

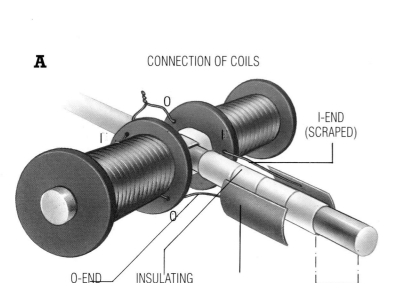

A CONNECTION OF COILS

O-END (SCRAPED
INSULATING TAPE
SEGMENT
I-END (SCRAPED)
⁵/₁₆" (8 mm)

1. Connect the outgoing wire of one coil with the incoming wire of the other. Do this by twisting the wires together (after you've scraped off the insulating enamel from the ends.) (Drawing A.)

2. Cover the long section of the shaft with insulating tape, but leave about ⁵/₁₆ inch (8 mm) bare at the end. Now, place commutator segments over the tape, one on either side of the shaft, with the free ends of the coils

B
INSULATING TAPE
SEGMENT
SEGMENT

tucked inside them (after removing the enamel), as shown in drawing A. Be sure that the commutator segments do not touch each other.

3. Carefully secure the segments close to the shaft using two of your thin strips of insulating tape. The photograph at right shows what the rotating part of your motor should look like after it has been assembled.

4. Prepare the motor brushes. (Drawing C.) It's easy: Make them from two pieces of single-strand wire, insulated or not, about 2¹/₂ inches (6 cm) long, with a hook at one end for attaching with a retainer screw to the wooden base. If you use insulated wire, you have to remove about ³/₄ inch (20 mm) of plastic from the end that is going to touch the segments.

C

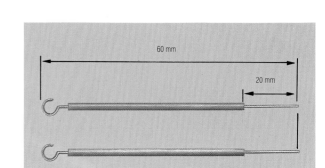

60 mm
20 mm

SIXTH STEP:
THE SHAFT SUPPORTS

Now we have to make two parts to support your motor shaft. These supports will allow the entire rotor assembly to turn. The following instructions give you only one idea, but there are obviously many ways of making a suitable support for a shaft. The important things are that the hole be at the correct height, that the hole have just the right diameter, and that the support be strong enough not to wobble with the movement of the motor. If you want to build our model, here are the instructions:

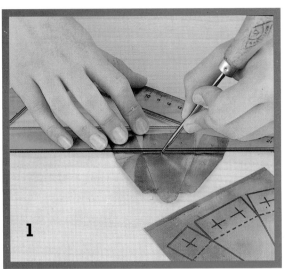

1

4

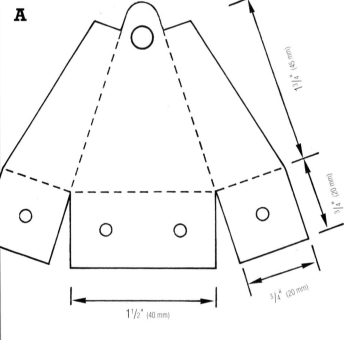

1. First, you have to cut two pieces of tinplate. Be sure to do it under adult supervision. Twice, draw the pattern shown in illustration A in felt-tip pen, and use a punch to score the drawings. Press hard enough to make a clear outline of the part. Look at photograph 1.

2. Mark the exact center of the holes with a cross in each support, and make the holes with the punch. Place each part on a piece of wood and strike with the hammer, but <u>be careful</u>. Don't try to do it with a single blow.

3. Using the rat-tail file, enlarge the holes to fit the diameters of the shaft and the retaining screws. Use the flat file to remove the burrs around the holes.

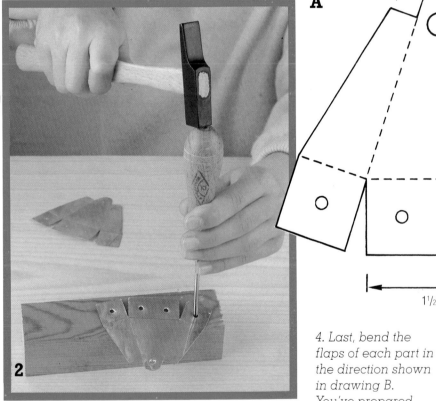

2

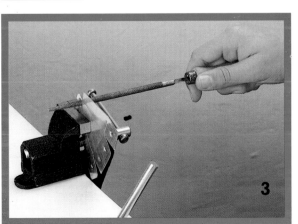

3

A

1 3/4" (45 mm)

3/4" (20 mm)

3/4" (20 mm)

1 1/2" (40 mm)

4. Last, bend the flaps of each part in the direction shown in drawing B. You've prepared the supports!

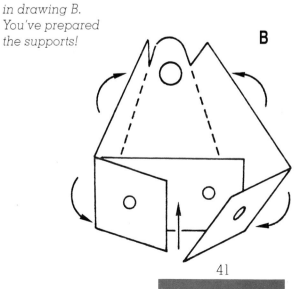

B

SEVENTH STEP:
PUTTING THINGS TOGETHER!

You've now made all the parts for your electric motor. You have the stator, the rotor with commutator, the shaft supports, and the two brushes.

All that remains for you to do is to correctly assemble these separate parts to form the motor. The list of materials calls for a wooden board. Now's the time to use it to secure all the different motor components.

Look at the drawing, it shows the wooden base, marking the places where the stator, the shaft supports, the two brushes, and the two connector terminals are to be screwed down.

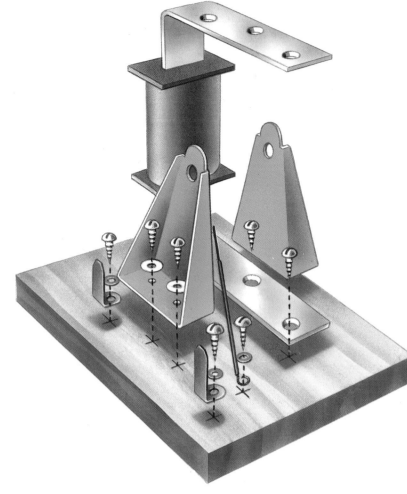

The drawing at right shows you the wooden board that acts as a base for our motor, and marks the position of the different parts. Although washers are essential where there is to be a connection, to insure better contact, you may also want to apply them to the shaft supports for extra steadiness.

In the photograph on the next page, you can see our motor running. We connected it to a 4.5-volt battery, but you can also connect it to a 9-volt one.

Naturally, we like to do a good job, so we've added some color by painting the shaft supports green and the cardboard washers for the rotor coil red. Also, we have used blue insulating tape to protect the stator coil.

Obviously, the last part you must fasten to the base is one of the shaft supports: When you have the shaft in the hole of the fastened support and the commutator between the two brushes, you can easily insert the other end of the shaft into the second support and screw the support in place.

CONNECT IT AND WATCH IT WORK!

Follow the diagram and instructions at right to make the connections between the different parts of the motor.

Make sure all the connections are properly made, check that the brushes touch the commutator segments (they should apply a slight pressure on them), connect your motor to a 4.5-volt battery (better if it's a new one), give the rotor blades a push and, if your motor starts right up, shout EUREKA!

If it refuses to start, don't worry:

- Check that all connection points are in good contact.
- Maybe you haven't scraped enough enamel from the ends of the copper wire of the coils.
- You may have wound one of the coils in the wrong direction.
- Make sure that the brushes touch the commutator segments and that there is enough pressure between them. This is very important.

CONCLUSION

The electric current causes the rotor and stator to become temporary magnets, each with a north and a south pole. Because—as you probably know—like poles repel and unlike poles attract, the south pole of the rotor is attracted to the north pole of the stator, making the rotor revolve half a turn. As the commutator segments have also revolved, the segment that touched the positive brush has now turned and made contact with the negative brush. This reverses the polarity of the rotor, which then gives another half turn. Therefore, while the current is turned on, it is the forces of attraction and repulsion that keep the rotor turning because the polarity is continually reversed.

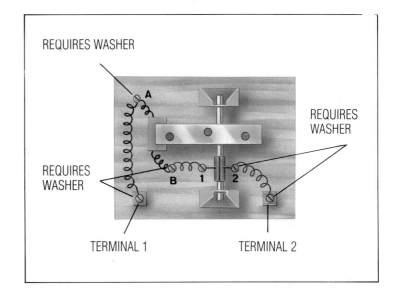

REQUIRES WASHER

REQUIRES WASHER

REQUIRES WASHER

A

B 1 2

TERMINAL 1 TERMINAL 2

The diagram shows how the motor is connected:
–First, connect end A of the rotor coil (in black) with one of the motor terminals.

–Connect end B of the rotor coil (in red) with brush 1.
–Last, connect brush 2 (also in red) to the other motor terminal.

IT'S THE IDEAS THAT COUNT!

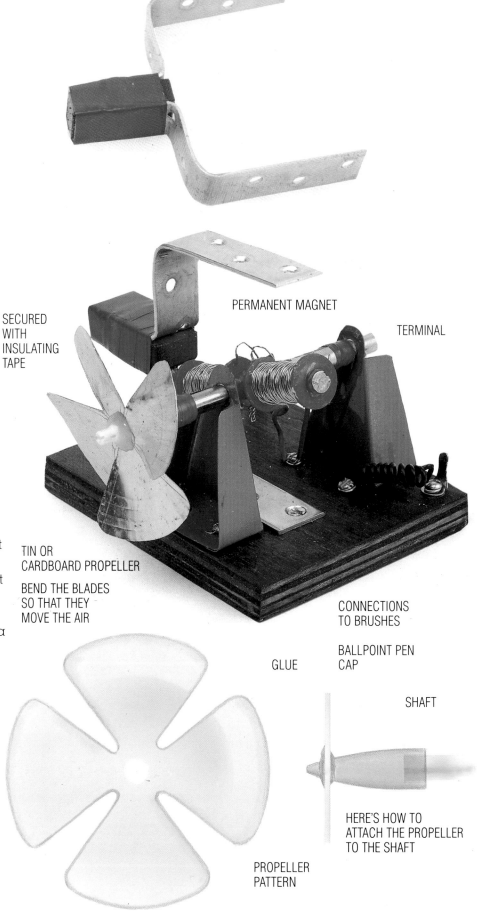

PERMANENT MAGNET

TERMINAL

SECURED WITH INSULATING TAPE

TIN OR CARDBOARD PROPELLER

BEND THE BLADES SO THAT THEY MOVE THE AIR

CONNECTIONS TO BRUSHES

BALLPOINT PEN CAP

GLUE

SHAFT

HERE'S HOW TO ATTACH THE PROPELLER TO THE SHAFT

PROPELLER PATTERN

Look what our friend is thinking! As he has a reasonably powerful permanent magnet, he has had the idea of making another motor, exactly the same as the last one, but with one difference: The stator, instead of being wound, uses a permanent magnet inserted between the two arms of the rotor, also called armature. On top of that, he made his motor useful by adding a propeller to the shaft, which could turn it into a small fan. What do you think?

HERE'S HIS IDEA

ARE YOU READY FOR A CHALLENGE?

A FINAL PIECE OF ADVICE: DON'T LET YOUR MOTORS WORK FOR TOO LONG. IT RUNS DOWN THE BATTERIES.

GLOSSARY

battery. A long-lasting source of electricity that produces energy through the chemical reaction of certain substances. One commonly used type is the wet cell battery, which uses acid and other substances. Another is the dry cell, which is not really dry, but contains chemicals in paste form. (See below.)

DRY-CELL BATTERY

chemical formula. A symbol that expresses the composition of a molecule of an element or compound. For example, the formula of water is H_2O. This means that a water molecule consists of two hydrogen atoms (H_2) and one oxygen atom (O). The letters correspond to the symbol of the chemical in question and the numbers tell you the number of atoms in each molecule.

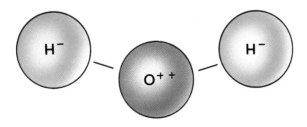

THE FORMULA OF WATER

The drawing above is the graphic way to express the formula of water. Each sphere represents an atom. Note the plus and minus symbols; these tell you that the oxygen atom, which has two positive electric charges, combines with two hydrogen atoms, each of which has one negative charge.

CONNECTOR TERMINALS

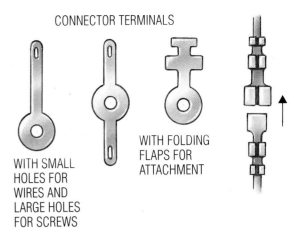

WITH SMALL HOLES FOR WIRES AND LARGE HOLES FOR SCREWS

WITH FOLDING FLAPS FOR ATTACHMENT

connector terminal. A small component used in electricity and electronics for easily establishing electric contact between conductors or between a conductor and an electric device. There are several types, to suit different purposes. The drawing above shows the most common terminals.

EFFECTS OF ELECTRIC CURRENT

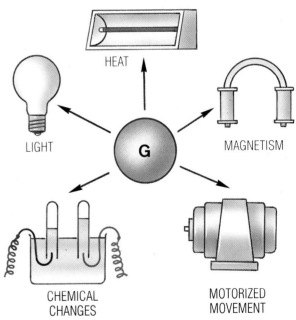

HEAT

LIGHT

G

MAGNETISM

CHEMICAL CHANGES

MOTORIZED MOVEMENT

effect. The result of any action or force. In electricity, the term can be applied to all that results from applying it. However, the basic effects that an electric current can produce are the following:
Calorific effects. Electricity produces heat.
Luminous effects. Electricity produces light.
Magnetic effects. Electricity produces magnetic force fields.
Chemical effects. Electricity can produce forces that, in turn, produce movement.

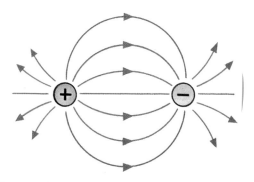

LINES OF FORCE
OF AN
ELECTRIC FIELD

electric field. A region in which an electric charge is distributed and where it acts upon other electric charges, forming invisible lines of force. See the drawing above. (See also *force field*.)

elements. In chemistry, those substances that are formed by a single type of atom. Substances formed by two or more elements are compounds. Water is a compound, formed by hydrogen and oxygen atoms. Both hydrogen and oxygen are gases, but when they are chemically combined they form a liquid compound.

force field. A region in which a force acts and where it traces an invisible pattern, which scientists call lines of force. (See *electric field*, *magnetic field*.)

generator. In electricity, a device that supplies electricity using a different type of energy. This term, used alone, usually refers to an electromagnetic generator, but it may be applied to other kinds. Here are some examples:

Electromagnetic generators: alternators and dynamos. These convert mechanical energy (for example, from a waterfall) into electricity.
Photoelectric generators. Devices, such as solar cells or photoelectric cells, that convert light into electricity.
Wind-driven electromagnetic generators. Alternators that use wind power to produce electricity. See the drawing below.

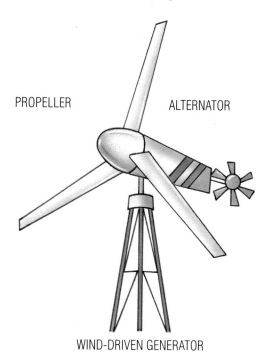

PROPELLER   ALTERNATOR

WIND-DRIVEN GENERATOR

ALTERNATOR
OR DYNAMO.
ELECTROMAGNETIC
GENERATOR

DAM

PLANT   PIPELINE

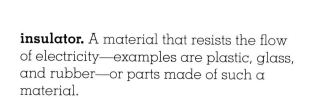

TURBINE

DIAGRAM OF A
HYDROELECTRIC
PLANT

insulator. A material that resists the flow of electricity—examples are plastic, glass, and rubber—or parts made of such a material.

LINES OF FORCE OF
THE EARTH'S
MAGNETIC FIELD

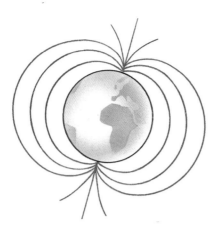

magnetic field. A region in which the force of a permanent magnet or electromagnet acts. As you probably know, the Earth acts like an enormous magnet, the poles of which are near Earth's geographic poles. Scientists believe that the lines of force of this large magnetic field surround our planet; they flow out of the south magnetic pole and return through the north magnetic pole. See the drawing above.

Using iron fillings, it is possible to make a *magnetic field picture* of either a bar or a horseshoe magnet: Place a piece of cardboard on top of a magnet; then, slowly sprinkle the surface with iron filings, and tap the card gently once or twice. You will see that the magnet acts on the filings, which then form a pattern along the magnet's lines of force, similar to the patterns shown in the drawings.

permanent magnet. A magnet that keeps its magnetism after the magnetizing force has been removed.

short circuit. As used in this book, an accidental connection in a circuit made between a conductor with less resistance and one that has the proper resistance to the amount of current flowing in the circuit. This will overheat the less resistant wires, which may melt and even start a fire.

temporary magnet. A magnet that has magnetic powers by electricity or by its proximity to another magnet, but loses its magnetism when the magnetizing force is removed.

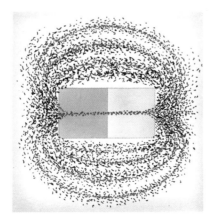

MAGNETIC FIELD PICTURE
OF A BAR MAGNET

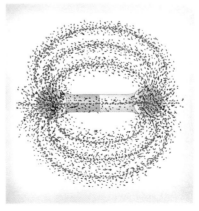

MAGNETIC FIELD PICTURE
OF A HORSESHOE MAGNET